FEATHERED FARM ANIMALS

TURKEYS

by Elizabeth Andrews

Cody Koala
An Imprint of Pop!
popbooksonline.com

Hello! My name is
Cody Koala

This book is filled with videos, puzzles, games, and more! Scan the QR codes* while you read, or visit the website below to make this book pop.

popbooksonline.com/turkey

*Scanning QR codes requires a web-enabled smart device with a QR code reader app and a camera.

abdobooks.com

Published by Pop!, a division of ABDO, PO Box 398166, Minneapolis, Minnesota 55439.

Printed in the United States of America, North Mankato, Minnesota.

082025
012026

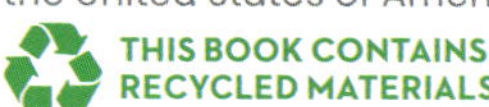

Cover Photo: Shutterstock Images
Interior Photos: Shutterstock Images; Getty Images
Editors: Tyler Gieseke and Grace Hansen
Series Designer: Julia Line

Library of Congress Control Number: 2025940513

Publisher's Cataloging-in-Publication Data
Names: Andrews, Elizabeth, author.
Title: Turkeys / by Elizabeth Andrews
Description: Minneapolis, Minnesota : Pop!, 2026 | Series: Feathered farm animals | Includes online resources and index
Identifiers: ISBN 9781098248581 (lib. bdg.) | ISBN 9781098249106 (ebook)
Subjects: LCSH: Turkeys--Juvenile literature. | Poultry--Juvenile literature. | Fowls--Juvenile literature. | Farm animals--Juvenile literature. | Animal husbandry--Juvenile literature.
Classification: DDC 636.592--dc23

Table of Contents

Chapter 1

Meet the Turkey!

Turkeys are birds. A group of **domestic** turkeys is called a rafter. Male turkeys are called toms. Female turkeys are called hens. Turkeys gobble. Farmers raise them for their meat.

Watch a video here!

Turkeys are large, round birds covered in feathers. The most common turkeys on

Some farmers sell turkey feathers and eggs too.

farms are broad-breasted white turkeys. Other turkeys can be many different colors.

Turkeys can grow to be 4 feet (1.2 m) tall. They weigh 17 to 30 pounds (7.7–13.6 kg). Hens are smaller than toms. Turkeys have sharp claws. They have a wattle and snood on their head.

tail
beak
snood
wattle
claw

Hens start laying eggs
at about seven months old.
They can lay 100 eggs a year!

Turkeys lay most of their eggs in the spring.

Turkey eggs are white with brown speckles. They are bigger than chicken eggs.

Chapter 2

Life on the Farm

Domestic turkeys live on farms. On large farms, they are kept in big barns at all times. On smaller farms, turkeys spend the day outside in pens or even **roaming** freely.

Learn more here!

Turkeys sleep in a **coop** or barn. This keeps them safe from **predators**. Turkeys also need low **roosts** in their sleeping areas. They like to sleep off the ground.

Domestic turkeys are too large to fly.

Chapter 3

What Do They Eat?

Turkeys who **roam** outside eat seeds, insects, and fruits. Turkeys living in large barns get **feed** made with grains and other **vitamins**. All turkeys need clean, fresh water daily.

Explore links here!

Chapter 4

Little Poults

Baby turkeys are called poults. They **hatch** from eggs. Poults are covered in soft feathers. They stay in a brooding house for eight weeks. This house keeps them safe and warm.

Complete an activity here!

Poults begin getting their adult feathers at around two months old. These feathers

keep them warm and dry. Poults join their rafter at around three months old.

Making Connections

Text-to-Self

What is one new thing you learned about turkeys in this book?

Text-to-Text

Have you read any other books about farm animals? How were those animals similar to or different from turkeys?

Text-to-World

Wild turkeys live in the United States. With the help of an adult, research places where wild turkeys live. Write a few sentences about how their lives may be different from those of domestic turkeys.

Glossary

coop – a small enclosed space to house farm birds.

domestic – tame and raised by humans; not wild.

feed – food designed for a specific kind of animal.

hatch – to break out of an egg.

predator – an animal that lives by hunting and eating other animals.

roam – to move freely without purpose or direction.

roost – a support on which birds rest.

vitamin – one of a number of natural or human-made substances needed to keep a body healthy.

Index

Online Resources

popbooksonline.com

Thanks for reading this Cody Koala book!

This book is filled with videos, puzzles, games, and more! Scan the QR codes* while you read, or visit the website below to make this book pop.

popbooksonline.com/turkey

*Scanning QR codes requires a web-enabled smart device with a QR code reader app and a camera.